EMBRACING WHOLENESS

MOTTOS AND AFFRIMATIONS FOR A HOLISTIC LIFE

BY KRISTINA ALAVANJA

WELCOME TO THE STORY BEHIND THE COVER

The cover of **"Embracing Wholeness: Mottos and Affirmations for a Holistic Life"** is a visual journey into self-discovery and personal growth. The central image features a hand gently releasing vibrant butterflies, symbolizing the transformative process of letting go and embracing life's lessons.

Each butterfly, unique in its colour and pattern, represents the diverse experiences and insights that shape our lives. The butterflies with patterns are coloured in vibrant hues like blues, yellows, and oranges, symbolizing joy, enthusiasm, and creativity. The butterflies without patterns are coloured in a single, simple colour, creating a beautiful contrast and emphasizing the uniqueness of each life lesson, quote, or message.

The flowers, scattered across the cover, are coloured in a mix of red, yellow, pink, blue, and violet. Each colour adds its own unique symbolism- love, romance, joy, gratitude, sincerity, unity, depth, stability, mystery, and creativity - resonating with the mottos and affirmations in the book.

The leaves, depicted in various shades of green, symbolize fertility and opulence, aligning with the theme of embracing wholeness and living a holistic life.

The background of the cover is white, signifying a fresh start and a blank canvas on which we paint our life's journey. This clean, minimalist backdrop allows the colours of the butterflies, flowers, and leaves to stand out, drawing the reader into the journey of self-discovery and personal growth that awaits within the pages of the book.

WELCOME TO YOUR CONTENT

EMBRACE THE POWER OF HOLISTIC AFFIRMATIONS AND MOTTOS

"Change your thoughts and change your world" – **Norman Vincent Peale.**

"Healing is a matter of time, but it is sometimes also a matter of opportunity." – **Hippocrates**

"The part can never be well unless the whole is well." – **Plato**

"Health is a state of complete harmony of the body, mind, and spirit." - **B.K.S. Iyengar**

These mottos and affirmations are not bound by time or place; they are timeless tools for motivation, health, success, and self-growth. Practicing these affirmations requires patience and consistency. Make them a part of your daily routine, let them seep into your consciousness, and watch as they transform your mindset and your life.

Remember, these affirmations and mottos are not prescriptive. They don't have a specific usage time such as day or night. Instead, they are there for you whenever you need them. Reach out to this book whenever you seek guidance or motivation.

The holistic affirmations and mottos: within these pages are more than just words; they are powerful catalysts for change. Whether you need motivation for health, success, or self-growth, these affirmations and mottos are here to empower and guide you on your journey.

let's embark on this transformative journey together. Let the power of holistic affirmations and mottos guide you towards a more empowered and inspired you. Remember, as **Norman Vincent Peale said, changing your thoughts can change your world. Let this book be the first step in** that transformation.

AFFIRMATIONS: A TOOL FOR POSITIVE CHANGE IN COGNITIVE BEHAVIOUR THERAPY

Evidence suggests that affirmations can positively impact an individual's overall well-being. However, it's important to remember that each person is unique, and achieving the desired outcome requires time and commitment. **Cognitive Behaviour Therapy (CBT)** provides evidence that it's possible to alter one's thought process using the right tools and techniques. Yet, patience, consistency, and time are crucial elements in this process.

Furthermore, an individual's psychological well-being plays a significant role. If a person is suffering from a psychological disorder, affirmations may not be effective during that period. It's essential first to address the disorder, possibly with medication and therapy. After achieving a balanced state of mind, it can be beneficial to implement holistic affirmations.

Affirmations are helpful and provide many benefits, but it is important to practice them daily and make them part of your life. In time, you will be able to do the affirmations subconsciously, and you won't need to refer to them.

When you are struggling psychologically, it is important that you reach out to a professional. We all struggle at times, and there is no need to feel ashamed. It is important that you take care of yourself and put yourself first, regardless of others' opinions.

You live your life for yourself. Don't ever hesitate to reach out when you need to just because of stigma. You're more important than what others think or believe.

Don't put your wellbeing in jeopardy. Just like your body needs a doctor, your mind also needs professional help. We are lucky to live in a world where we can finally treat both our bodies, our minds, heart, and soul."

THE POWER OF REPETITION

AFFRIMATIONS FOR LIFE

In this book, you'll notice that each affirmation has its own section and title. This is designed to give each affirmation its own space and importance. However, you'll also see that some affirmations are repeated in different sections. This is intentional. The repetition is meant to underscore the importance of these affirmations and to remind you that they can be applied in various aspects of your life, regardless of the section title. Moreover, I've chosen to add a creative touch by writing a story behind the cover. This story serves as a preview of what's inside the book, giving you a glimpse of its contents before you even begin reading.

As a writer, my goal is to inspire, empower, and heal people through the art of words and colours. When you look at the cover and start reading, you'll find that the style is quite different from what you may have read before. This book is all about bringing positive benefits to you and making the words stand out enough to make a difference in your life. Remember, the power of affirmations lies in their repetition. So, don't hesitate to revisit these affirmations as often as you need.

UNDERSTANDING THE IMPORTANCE OF GUIDELINES BEFORE PRACTICING AFFIRMATIONS

Before we dive into the world of affirmations, it's crucial to understand the importance of following certain guidelines. These guidelines are designed to maximize the effectiveness of your affirmation practice and ensure a positive and enriching experience.

THE ROLE OF GUIDELINESS

Guidelines act as a roadmap, leading you towards the correct and effective use of affirmations. They help you avoid common pitfalls and misconceptions, ensuring that your journey with affirmations is smooth and beneficial.

IMPORTANCE OF ADHERENCE

Adhering to these guidelines is not a mere formality. It's a vital step in preparing your mind and setting the right intentions. This preparation is key to unlocking the full potential of affirmations.

WHAT TO EXPECT

In the following chapters, we will introduce these guidelines in detail. We will discuss each guideline, its purpose, and the role it plays in your affirmation practice.

CONCLUSION

Remember, the journey of a thousand miles begins with a single step. Understanding and following these guidelines is that first crucial step in your journey towards self-improvement and actualization through affirmations.

In the next chapter, we will begin introducing the affirmations. Until then, familiarize yourself with these guidelines and prepare your mind for the journey ahead.

EFFECTIVE USE OF HOLISTIC AFFRIMATIONS

✓ **Identify Negative Thoughts:** Recognize the negative thought patterns and beliefs that you want to change.

✓ **Create Positive Affirmations:** Replace these negative thoughts with positive affirmations that resonate with you.

✓ **Practice Regularly**: Consistency is key. Practice your affirmations daily, ideally at the same time each day.

✓ **Patience:** Changes won't happen overnight. Be patient with yourself and the process.

✓ **Seek Professional Help if Needed**: If you're dealing with a psychological disorder, seek professional help. After achieving a balanced state of mind, you can incorporate affirmations into your routine."

AFFRIMATIONS FOR POSITIVE THINKING

- Today is a new day, and I will start it with a positive thought.

- I will pay more attention to the beautiful scenery around me, rather than always focusing on work and what I need to do. I will enjoy the simplicity and beauty of nature.

- I am more confident today than I was yesterday, and each day I will become more confident and improve in the areas of my life with which I struggle the most.

- Today, I will be open to new opportunities. I won't allow fear to invade my mind and take away my possibilities for a good life, health, and success.

- I know that there is good in every situation. By changing the way, I think, I can see more clearly and understand the bigger picture.

- Today, I will get up, stretch, feel refreshed, smile, breathe in fresh air, have my tea or cup of coffee, and take on today with positive energy and excitement.

- At the end of every day, or as often as possible, I will prioritize myself. I will have a self-care day/night because I am worthy of it and I deserve it.

- I will love and appreciate who I am every day because I am amazing.

- At the end of each day, when I get home or finish my work for that day, I will say thank you because I lived another day, no matter the situation I was in.

- Every day, I will be grateful for what I have.
- To the best of my ability, I will make the right choices for myself.
- I will tell myself every day, "Today you did well, you're a great person, you did the best that you could have done in that moment. You will improve every day, don't be too hard on yourself, you're only human, just keep trying.

SELF- LOVE AND HEALING

- Loving and respecting myself will be my top priority. Self-love is the most important love that I can give to myself.

- I can achieve anything that I put my mind to. It is easy to say, "I can't," or to ask, "Is this possible?" Changing my mindset will get me to where I want to be in life.

- Believing in myself is the key to success. Self-belief is a driving force not just for success but for everything else I want to achieve and experience in life.

- I won't allow the opinions of others to affect my confidence and my self-worth. What I think about myself is what is important.

- I am not a failure. I am a success waiting to happen. Positive thinking will create a positive outcome.

- To fail is okay; to give up is not okay. I will fail; it's part of life, but I won't ever say, "I can't," because it doesn't exist in my vocabulary.

- I will stand up and move on, keep fighting until I achieve what I desire.

- I will love myself even if I don't like myself at times.

- I deserve the best that this world can offer. At times, I am hard on myself, but I know that I deserve good things and that I am worth it.

- Toxic people don't belong in my life. People who wish me

harm are not welcome. I know my worth.

- I am hurting, and at times it feels like it will never end. All I must remember is that every start has an ending.
- I will like and love who I see when I look at myself in the mirror.
- Pain and trauma will change me. I will never be the same, but I will be the one who will choose how I will allow it to change me. I won't choose to be angry, to be bitter, to be mean, to harm myself, or to isolate myself.
- I will take care of my physical, psychological, emotional, and spiritual well-being.
- In time, I will get better. All I need is time, patience, commitment, and determination. At the end of my healing journey, I will get my reward, and it will be worth it.
- I will think before I act, understanding that every action has a reaction, either positive or negative. Either way, those are the reactions that I will have to live with.
- It's okay to not be okay. No feeling is permanent. This too shall pass.
- Self-care will be a part of my daily routine.
- I experience the traumas of life, but I also know that I have everything that I need to start my healing journey and to stand again on my two feet. Finally, I am okay, maybe not like before, but I am okay. I am alive.
- I am still standing, I am a fighter, and I am a survivor. I will survive the storms of life.
- I will stop worrying about everything. I will focus on what I can control and what I can't allow to enter my mind.

AFFRIMATIONS FOR CREATIVIETY

- I have a natural talent for creativity. My passion and belief empower and inspire me, and my belief in my talent drives me to be creative.
- I will seize every opportunity to open my creative mind and use my hands to create to the best of my ability.
- Everything and everyone around me can be my creative muse. There is inspiration all around me; all I need to do is be open and allow it to become a part of me.
- Every day, I become more and more creative. By nurturing my creative side, I can dive deeper and discover new creative ideas and excitement.
- I will listen to my mind, body, heart, and soul. If I am not inspired or if it is not the right time, it is important that I take a break and not force it. My creative side also needs a break. I will go with the flow.
- Sometimes, I draw outside the lines, and that's okay. Creativity is not about perfection; it is about the expression of emotions, talents, and ideas.
- My imagination and passion drive my creativity.
- I use everything around me and pour it into my art, photography, crafting, writing. Everything I touch enforces my creative side.
- To create or not to create, it will always be to create, just like

to be or not to be, it will always be.

- I am an author of my own creation.
- My creative gifts influence others by evoking their imagination and creative side, opening the communication between art and their emotions.
- I won't allow negativity to influence my creativity.
- I am open to new ideas and experiences, allowing them to stir my creative spirit and inspire my work.
- I trust in my creative process, knowing that each step I take is bringing me closer to my artistic vision.
- I celebrate my unique perspective and creativity, understanding that my individuality is my greatest strength in my artistic endeavours.

POSITIVE AFFRIMATIONS FOR EVERYDAY

- Today is a new day, and I will start it with a positive thought.
- I will pay more attention to the beautiful scenery around me, rather than always focusing on work and what I need to do. I will enjoy the simplicity and beauty of nature.
- I am more confident today than I was yesterday, and each day I will become more confident and improve in the areas of my life with which I struggle the most.
- Today, I will be open to new opportunities. I won't allow fear to invade my mind and take away my possibilities for a good life, health, and success.
- I know that there is good in every situation. By changing the way, I think, I can see more clearly and understand the bigger picture.
- Today, I will get up, stretch, feel refreshed, smile, breathe in fresh air, have my tea or coffee, and take on today's day with positive energy and excitement.
- At the end of every day, or as often as possible, I will prioritize myself. I will have a self-care day/night because I am worthy of it and I deserve it.
- I will love and appreciate who I am every day because I am amazing.
- At the end of each day, when I get home or finish my work for

that day, I will say thank you because I lived another day, no matter the situation I was in.

- Every day, I will be grateful for what I have.
- To the best of my ability, I will make the right choices for myself.
- I will tell myself every day, "Today you did well. You're a great person. You did the best that you could have done in that moment.

HEALING OF MIND, BODY, SPIRIT

- I am open to the natural flow of wellness now.
- My body knows how to heal itself, and is doing so even now.
- My body, mind, and spirit are vibrant and healthy.
- Every cell in my body vibrates with energy and health.
- I am whole, healthy, and strong.
- I am grateful for the healing happening in my body now.
- I love taking care of myself.
- Today, every cell in my body is functioning perfectly.
- I feel the glow of God's love in every cell of my body.
- I am radiant, beautiful and strong, and enjoy a healthy and passionate life.
- I have a special guardian angel. I am divinely guided and protected at all times.
- Perfect health is my divine right, and I claim it now.
- I am grateful for the opportunity to balance my mind, body, and spirit.
- I release all disease from my body and welcome health, love, and happiness into my life.
- I am constantly discovering new ways to improve my health.
- I enjoy exercising my body and strengthening my muscles.
- With every heartbeat, I am more and more healthy.
- Every fibre of my being radiates positive energy.
- I am grateful for my healthy body and mind.

- I do not fear being unhealthy because I know that I control my own body.
- I am always able to maintain my ideal weight.
- I am filled with energy to do all the daily activities in my life.
- My mind is at peace.
- I love and care for my body and it cares for me.
- I have abundant energy, vitality and well-being.
- I am always able to maintain my ideal weight.
- I am filled with energy to do all the daily activities in my life.

AFFRIMATIONS FOR MOTIVATION

- **Embrace the Challenge**: I am capable of overcoming any obstacles that come my way.
- **Growth and Progress**: Every day, in every way, I am becoming better and better.
- **Self-Belief:** I believe in myself and my ability to succeed.
- **Persistence Pays Off:** I am persistent and will never quit.
- **Embrace the Journey:** I enjoy the journey and strive to constantly improve.
- **Positivity is Power:** I am a positive thinker, and I attract positive circumstances.
- **Limitless Potential:** I acknowledge my own self-worth; my potential to succeed is infinite.
- **Fear is Temporary:** I let go of my fears and move forward with courage and confidence.
- **Resilience:** I have the power to overcome adversity. My challenges make me stronger.
- **Success Mindset**: Success is my natural state, and I expect to be successful in all of my endeavours.
- **Gratitude Attitude:** I am grateful for every day and the opportunities it brings.
- **Vision and Goal:** I am committed to my goals and my vision for success.
- **Inner Strength:** I have the strength to make my dreams come

true.

- **Action and Initiative:** I take action and make things happen.
- **Learning and Knowledge:** I am always learning and growing.
- **Health and Well-being:** I am healthy, energetic, and full of vitality.
- **Harmony and Balance:** I live in harmony with myself and others.
- **Creativity and Innovation:** I am full of new ideas and creativity.
- **Kindness and Love:** I spread love and kindness wherever I go.
- **Patience and Understanding:** I am patient and understanding with myself and others.

AFFRIMATIONS FOR STRESS AND ANXIETY

- I acknowledge my anxiety, but I do not give it the power to hurt me or control me.
- I can identify the difference between my rational and irrational thoughts. This gives me the power to control my anxiety.
- I am calm because I choose to be.
- I am in control of my breathing.
- I will start my day with a positive mindset. This will help ease and control my anxiety.
- I am safe, I am okay, everything will be just fine.
- I am strong and capable of managing my anxiety when it is triggered, with calmness.
- A positive thought a day can manifest a positive outcome.
- I am a survivor. I have survived many hardships. Anxiety is nothing compared to everything else I went through. I am a fighter.
- I will only let positive people into my life, people who love me and wish me well. I will never allow negative, toxic people to enter my life, my mind, or my heart.
- When I feel stressed, I will stop, close my eyes, take a few breaths in through my nose and out through my mouth until I feel my mind and body calming down. With a positive

attitude, I will start my day.

- I will take care of my mental and physical health.
- For my own peace of mind and wellbeing, I won't allow others' opinions to influence me in a negative sense. I won't take things personally.
- When I need to, I will reach out for help from family, friends, and professionals.

AFFIRMATIONS FOR SUCCESS

- I can succeed in everything that I put my mind to. All I need is to believe in myself. That's where the most important success comes from.
- I find it easy to succeed because I am driven, passionate, determined, and have self-belief.
- I am committed to succeeding, knowing that there will be obstacles in my way.
- I see every small step as a success. Every small step leads me to big success.
- I am open when it comes to taking risks because without risks there is no success.
- Every small success is something to be proud of. I am proud of myself and my accomplishments.
- Positive thinking is the main key towards becoming successful in my goal.
- I am resilient and can bounce back from any setbacks. Challenges are opportunities for growth and learning.
- I am deserving of success. My hard work and dedication will pay off.
- I am focused on my goals and will not be distracted by obstacles.
- I am constantly improving and striving to do my best.
- I am grateful for every opportunity that comes my way.

- I am confident in my abilities and skills.
- I am not afraid of failure. It's not a setback, but a setup for a comeback.
- I am patient and persistent in my pursuit of success.
- I am worthy of all the good things that happen in my life.
- I trust in my ability to create a successful future.

DEPRESSION: UNDERSTANDING, COPING, AND FINDING STRENGHT

"**Depression is a serious psychological disorder**: often brought on by overwhelming life events and traumas. It's not simply a state of feeling sad or 'blue', but a condition that affects every aspect of a person's life, from their thoughts and feelings to their physical health. It's important to remember that depression is not a sign of weakness or something that can be overcome with willpower alone. It's a real, medical condition that requires professional treatment, just like any other health issue.

If you or someone you know is struggling with depression, it's crucial to reach out for help. There's no need to face this alone, and there are many resources available, including mental health professionals and support groups.

The affirmations in this section are designed to serve as a source of positivity and strength. They are not a substitute for professional help, but they can be a powerful tool in your mental health toolkit. As you read them, remember that it's okay to ask for help, and it's okay to take care of yourself. You are not alone in this journey."

AFFRIMATIONS FOR DEPRESSION

> I acknowledge my depression, but I do not allow it to define me.

> I am more than my depression. I am strong, resilient, and capable.

> I am deserving of love, peace, and happiness.

> I am not alone in my feelings, and I am okay with asking for help.

> I am in control of my life and my path to healing.

> I am patient with myself and recognize that healing takes time.

> I am focused on positive thoughts and actions that uplift my spirit.

> I am kind to myself and give myself the care that I need.

> I am surrounded by love and support.

> I am taking steps each day to overcome my depression.

> I am hopeful about my future and look forward to each new day.

> I am not defined by my depression. I am defined by my strength and kindness.

> I am worthy of love and joy.

> I choose to focus on the things that make me feel good.

> I have the power to change my thoughts, and I am becoming more positive each day.

> I am proud of myself for facing and overcoming my challenges.

> I am becoming stronger and more resilient every day.

> I am capable of creating the life that I desire.

> I am deserving of all the beauty that life has to offer.

> I am surrounded by people who love and support me.

> I am doing the best I can, and that is enough.

> I am learning to love and accept myself unconditionally.

> I am brave for facing my fears and continuing to fight.

> I am taking steps each day to nourish my mind, body, and soul.

> I am finding joy in the small moments.

> I am not alone in my struggles and it's okay to ask for help.

> I am patient with my healing process and acknowledge
that it takes time.

LET'S DISCOVER

A Holistic Approach to Self-Growth and Empowerment." This section is a collection of mottos that serve as guiding principles in the journey of life. They are not just words, but powerful tools for inspiration, empowerment, and self-growth.

The essence of this book lies in its holistic approach. It's about learning about yourself through your own experiences and through the eyes of others. It's about understanding that every interaction, every piece of advice, every success, and every failure is an opportunity for growth and learning.

Throughout our lives, we receive advice from various sources - friends, family, grandparents. Sometimes we take this advice into consideration, sometimes we don't. Each decision, whether to follow the advice or not, leads us down a different path. Each path, in turn, offers its own lessons and experiences.

This book encourages you to reflect on these experiences. Did you take the advice from your loved ones? How did it go? What did you learn from the experience? What happened when you decided not to take the advice? Did you learn something then?

The mottos in this book are derived from such life experiences. They are nuggets of wisdom that can help guide your actions and decisions. They are reminders that every experience, every interaction, is a step in the journey of self-growth.

As you read through these mottos, I invite you to reflect on your own life experiences. Consider how these mottos resonate with you, how they apply to your life, and how they can guide you in your journey of self-growth and empowerment.

NAVIGATING LIFE'S JOURNEY: MOTTOS FOR PERSONAL GROWTH

"Welcome to 'Navigating Life's Journey: Mottos for Personal Growth'. This collection of advice and mottos is a reflection of my own journey through life. It's important to remember that these insights are subjective, born from my personal experiences and observations. However, I firmly believe in the power of shared wisdom. We all learn from one another, and it's my hope that these words might resonate with you, inspire you, or offer a new perspective.

As you read, I invite you to reflect on your own experiences and consider how these mottos might apply to your life. Remember, the journey of personal growth is unique for everyone. Here's to navigating life's journey together."

SECTION 1:
PERSONAL GROWTH

- You are the only one who can make yourself happy, be a creator of your own happiness.
- Be better than you were yesterday, always work towards self-improvement.
- It's never too late to be who you want to be, to grow, to live, to learn.
- If you can think negatively, you sure can invest to think in a positive manner as well.
- Be your own friend, once you are you will always do right by you.
- You choose yourself and your own happiness.
- You know that you can't achieve everything, but you will make sure that for you, impossible becomes possible.
- Change is the only constant in life. Embrace it, adapt to it, and grow with it.

SECTION 2:
LEARNING FROM LIFE

- Leave the regrets in the past, those won't help your present and future.
- Learn from your mistakes and use them as a life lesson.
- Even when I am defeated, I can choose to learn from it.
- My mistakes are the lessons waiting to be learned.
- Every pain in life can teach you a lesson.
- You will learn not just from happiness but from pain.
- With every step that you take in this world, it's the mark that you leave.
- Even the darkest night will pass, and the sun will rise. Keep going, your dawn is coming

SECTION 3:
MINDFULNESS AND
SELF- CARE

- Learn how to stop and breathe, be in a moment, just breathe and focus on that.
- Laughter is a medicine for the soul but so is crying.
- Give value to your sorrows not just to your happiness, we can learn a lot from our pain.
- Loving yourself is the most beautiful love you can ever experience in your life.
- Take breaks, it is essential for your wellbeing.

- When happiness finds you, grab it with both arms.
- Trust your instincts. They're a culmination of your experiences and wisdom guiding you.

SECTION 4:
NAVIGATING
RELATIONSHIPS
AND INTERACTIONS

- Be who you want to be not what somebody else thinks that you should be.
- When you get rejected don't take it personally, it has nothing to do with you.
- If you don't respect and value yourself, nobody else will.
- In this life you will be treated the way you treat others, if you want to be treated with love and respect then treat others the same way.
- You can't please everyone, so stop trying.
- You won't allow the opinions of others to affect your confidence and your self-worth. What you think about yourself is what is important.
- Toxic people don't belong in your life. People who wish you harm are not welcome. You know your worth.

SECTION 5:
EMBRACING LIFE'S
JOURNEY

❖ You can't control life plan for you, but you can learn how to control how you react.

❖ A long road taken is never easy, it comes with many obstacles but what's waiting for you at the end is worth it, so climb, walk, reach, succeed, enjoy.

❖ Life is all about choices and every choice has a consequence, either good or bad.

❖ If you don't like your life, then change it.

❖ The best way to predict your future is to create it.

❖ You are still standing, you are a fighter, and you are a survivor. You will survive the storms of life.

❖ You will stop worrying about everything. You will focus on what you can control and what you can't allow to enter your mind.

❖ You have power over your own mind. Not every thought in your head is real. Some are just part of insecurities which you can work on and improve.

❖ You can run but you can't hide. Fight your inner demons with a sword. You're the only one who can win them, you know your own enemies.

THE RATIONALE
BEHIND THE
MOTTOS

"In my quest to explore the vast spectrum of human thought and wisdom, I decided to include famous people's mottos in my book. While I have my own philosophies and beliefs, I felt that incorporating the mottos of renowned individuals would add a layer of diversity and creativity to the narrative. These mottos, which have guided the lives of many influential figures, offer unique perspectives and insights that enrich the content.

They serve as a testament to the myriad ways in which we perceive and navigate our world, thereby fostering a more comprehensive understanding of life's complexities. By juxtaposing these mottos with my own, I hope to create a dynamic interplay of ideas that resonates with a wide range of readers and sparks meaningful conversations."

SECTION 6:
OVERCOMING FEAR
AND DOUBT

- "True terror is to wake up one morning and discover that your high school class is running the country." *- Kurt Vonnegut*
- "Sometimes the road less travelled is less travelled for a reason." *- Jerry Seinfeld*
- "When in doubt, stand still." *- Julie Andrews*
- "Those who dare to fail miserably can achieve greatly." *- John F.* Kennedy
- "The future belongs to those who prepare for it today."*- Malcolm X*

SECTION 7: FINDING HAPPINESS AND MEANING

- "Always forgive your enemies; nothing annoys them so much." - *Oscar Wilde*
- "This above all: to thine own self be true." - *Hugh Hefner*
- "I am part of god in light." - *Shirley MacLaine*
- "Keep smiling and maybe you'll get something to smile about." - *Yoko Ono*
- "All that we are is the result of what we have thought." - *Buddha*
- "If you judge people, you have no time to love them." - *Mother Teresa*
- "The greatest wealth is to live content with little." – *Plato*

SECTION 8:
GROWING AND
LEARNING

- "Never go to bed mad. Stay up and fight." - _Phyllis Diller_
- "If you can't be kind, at least be vague." - _Judith Martin_
- "Be cool." - _Brian Wilson_
- "The most courageous act is still to think for yourself. Aloud." - _Coco Chanel_
- "I have no special talent. I am only passionately curious." - _Albert_ Einstein
- "The successful warrior is the average man, with laser-like focus." _- Bruce Lee_
- "A great man is always willing to be little." - _Ralph Waldo Emerson_
- "Wisely, and slow. They stumble that run fast." _- William_ Shakespeare
- "What you do makes a difference, and you have to decide what kind of difference you want to make." - _Jane Goodall_
- "Stay afraid, but do it anyway. What's important is the action. You don't have to wait to be confident. Just do it and eventually the confidence will follow." - _Carrie Fisher_
- "One can choose to go back toward safety or forward toward growth. Growth must be chosen again and again; fear must be overcome again and again." - _Abraham Maslow_
- "The swiftest way to triple your success is to double your

investment in personal development." - *Robin Sharma*

INTRODUCTION TO ACTIVITY

This activity involves mottos and affirmations. Each motto or affirmation is a sentence with a missing word or phrase. Your task is to think about what word or phrase would be most meaningful to you in the context of the sentence.

SECTION 6: OVERCOMING FEAR AND DOUBT

I nstructions

1. Read each motto or affirmation carefully.

2. Reflect on what word or phrase would be most meaningful to you in the context of the sentence.

3. In your personal notebook or journal, write down the complete sentence with your chosen words or phrases.

Here are the mottos and affirmations for this activity:

1. A certain quality is the key to success.
2. I am a certain quality enough to handle whatever comes.
3. Every day in every way, I am getting a certain quality.

Remember, there are no right or wrong answers. The most important thing is that your responses resonate with you and help you to overcome fear and doubt. Enjoy the activity.

SECTION 7: FINDING HAPPINESS AND MEANING

I ntroduction

This activity involves a series of statements related to happiness and meaning. Each statement is a sentence with a missing word or phrase. Your task is to think about what word or phrase would be most meaningful to you in the context of the sentence.

Instructions

1. Read each statement carefully.

2. Reflect on what word or phrase would be most meaningful to you in the context of the sentence.

3. Write down the complete sentence with your chosen words or phrases in your personal notebook or journal.

Here are the statements for this activity:

1. I am in charge of my own certain quality.
2. I choose to focus on a certain quality.
3. I am becoming more of a certain quality every day.
4. I am thankful for a certain quality.
5. I have the power to do a certain action.

Remember, there are no right or wrong answers. The most important thing is that your responses resonate with you and help you to find happiness and meaning in your life. Enjoy the activity! ☺

Upon completing these activities, I hope you found them enjoyable and stimulating. These exercises are designed not only to keep your mind engaged but also to promote critical thinking. They offer a platform for self-discovery, allowing you to explore your thoughts and feelings in a structured way. Remember, the journey of self-discovery is ongoing, and these activities are just one of many tools you can use. Keep exploring, keep discovering, and most importantly, enjoy the process."

INTRODUCTION TO THE MOTTO ART ACTIVITY

In this activity, I invite you to create a piece of art that represents a motto that resonates with you. This could be a drawing, a collage, or even a sculpture. The art doesn't have to be a literal representation of the motto. It could be abstract, using colours, shapes, and textures to convey the feeling or idea behind the motto.

For example, if your personal motto is **"Embrace Change"**, you might create a piece of art that uses swirling colours and dynamic shapes to represent the concept of change and transformation.

After you've created your art, use this space to write about your artwork. What motto did you choose? Why does it resonate with you? How does your art represent this motto? Reflecting on these questions will help deepen your connection to your personal mottos.

Remember, there's no right or wrong way to do this activity. It's all about self-expression and exploring your personal motto in a creative way. **Enjoy the process!**

EMBRACING GROWTH AND SELF – LOVE

I trust that you have found value in the affirmations and mottos shared in this book. May they serve as guiding lights in your life, illuminating your path towards personal growth and self-love. It is my sincere belief that the wisdom encapsulated in these pages will inspire you to approach life with an open mind and heart. Remember, every person who enters your life has something to teach you, and every experience, a lesson to impart. Affirmations have the power to transform not just our thoughts, but our actions and lives. As you apply these affirmations and mottos, may you discover a newfound love and appreciation for yourself. After all, you are worth it.

Self-reflection is essential for self-growth, discovery, and self-love. Just like you would take care of your body, it is important that you also take care of your mind, heart, and spirit. We are lucky that we are living in the 21st century. Technology and medicine have improved not just for our body from a medical perspective, but also from a psychological and spiritual perspective.

Affirmations are proven to work. Affirmations are part of Cognitive Behaviour Therapy. It works by alternating your negative thoughts into more positive ones. By using affirmations, it also helps you with a range of things, such as confidence, calm mind, body, and soul. It can assist you in having a less stressful life, a life which is a bit easier to manage and function on a day-to-day basis. It helps you by engaging in certain activities or experiences can trigger the release of endorphins in the brain.

What is really important is to be productive, create a routine, follow that structure, and stay committed and patient. Believe in it, in time it will return its gratitude to you. Using affirmations, like I said, is like cognitive behaviour therapy. However, it's important to note that while affirmations can be a useful tool, they are typically used as part of a larger therapeutic process in CBT. When you think about Affirmations and CBT, connect it with: positive thinking, and positive emotions, also positive attitude, and life. Because that's what affirmations and CBT provide you with."

Now that you have been introduced to the transformative power of affirmations and Cognitive Behaviour Therapy, it's time to reflect on what you've learned. Remember, the journey of self-love and personal growth is a continuous process, not a destination.

As you close this chapter, take a moment to appreciate your commitment to self-improvement. You've taken the first step towards a more positive and fulfilling life.

In the coming days, I encourage you to apply the principles and practices discussed in this chapter. Observe the changes in your thoughts, attitudes, and actions. Remember, every small step counts.

Thank you for embarking on this journey with me. I hope that the insights and affirmations shared in this chapter will serve as a beacon of light, guiding you towards a path of self-love and personal growth.

Remember, you are worth it. Embrace growth, love yourself, and keep shining."

Best Wishes - Kristina Alavanja

THE POWER OF AFFRIMATIONS AND COGNITIVE BEHAVIOUR THERAPY TOOLS FOR PERSONAL GROWTH AND SELF-LOVE

The concept of affirmations has been around for thousands of years, with evidence of their use dating back to ancient civilizations like the Egyptians. However, they gained popularity in the early 20th century. Some believe that French author Emile Coué was the first to champion their use, while others credit self-help guru Napoleon Hill1. Affirmations were also used in spiritual or religious practices across many cultures and religions1. The term "affirmation" was first recorded in 1843 by philosopher and theologian Ralph Waldo Emerson.

As for **Cognitive Behaviour Therapy (CBT)**, it was pioneered by Dr. Aaron T. Beck in the 1960s 345. He developed this therapy as a way to recognize and change negative thought patterns and behaviors5. His work with depressed patients led him to develop a new theory of depression, focused on underlying negative beliefs associated with loss and failure.

PIONEERS OF POSITIVE CHANGE: THE LIVES AND WORKS OF EMILE COUE NAPOLEONE HILL, RALPH WALDO EMERSON, AND DR. ARON T. BECK

Emile Coué (1857-1926): Coué was a French psychologist and pharmacist who introduced a popular method of psychotherapy and self-improvement based on optimistic autosuggestion. He was born in Troyes, France, and initially intended to become an analytical chemist. However, he eventually decided to become a pharmacist and graduated with a degree in pharmacology in 18761. He discovered what later came to be known as the placebo effect while working as an apothecary at Troyes from 1882 to 19101.

Napoleon Hill (1883-1970): Hill was an American author best known for his book "Think and Grow Rich" (1937), which is among the best-selling self-help books of all time. He was born in a small cabin in Virginia and his works insisted that fervid expectations are essential to improving one's life. His contributions to the field of mental health and the tangible impact he had on the lives of so many people are astonishing.

Ralph Waldo Emerson (1803-1882): Emerson was an American essayist, lecturer, philosopher, abolitionist, and poet who led the transcendentalist movement of the mid-19th century. He was seen as a champion of individualism and critical thinking, as well as a prescient critic of the countervailing pressures of society and conformity. Emerson's "nature" was more philosophical than naturalistic

Dr. Aaron T. Beck (1921-2021): Beck was an American psychiatrist and a professor in the department of psychiatry at the University of Pennsylvania. He is regarded as the father of cognitive therapy and cognitive behavioural therapy (CBT). His pioneering methods are widely used in the treatment of clinical depression and various anxiety disorders. He also developed self-report measures for depression and anxiety, notably

"As we reflect on the lives and works of Emile Coué, Napoleon Hill, Ralph Waldo Emerson, and Dr. Aaron T. Beck, we see a common thread of dedication to understanding and improving the human mind. Their pioneering efforts have laid the foundation for the practices of affirmations and CBT that we know today. Their legacy continues to inspire countless individuals on their journey towards personal growth and self-love."

ESSENTIALS OF AFFRIMATIONS AND COGNITIVE BEHAVIOUR

BOOKS ON CBT

- "Cognitive Behaviour Therapy: Basics and Beyond" **by Judith S. Beck**
- "Learning Cognitive-Behaviour Therapy: An Illustrated Guide" **by Jesse H. Wright, Gregory K. Brown, Michael E. Thase, and Monica Ramirez Basco**
- "Cognitive-Behavioural Therapy" **by Michelle G. Craske**

BOOKS ON AFFRIMATIONS

❖ "Banish Your Self-Esteem Thief" **by Kate Collins-Donnelly**

❖ "Positive Affirmations: Daily affirmations for attracting health, healing, & happiness into your life" **by Rachel Robins**

❖ "365 Days of Positive Affirmations" **by Nicole Lockhart**

ONLINE COURSES
ON CBT

> "Cognitive Behavioural Therapy (CBT) Practitioner Course" **on Udemy**

> "Cognitive Behaviour Therapy (CBT)" **on health direct**

> "CBT Cognitive Behavioural Therapy" **courses on Udemy**

> Various CBT courses **on Coursera**

ONLINE COURSES ON AFFRIMATIONS

- "The Best Affirmation Class in the World" on Udemy
- "Positive Self Talk - Affirmations & Mindset" on Udemy
- "Positive Affirmations - For Daily Self Talk" on Udemy
- "Affirmations for Healing" on Ananda India Online

INSPIRING WORDS: FAMOUS AFFRIMATIONS AND QUOTES FROM RENOWNED FIGURES

Is a collection of powerful affirmations and insightful quotes from well-known personalities and professionals in various fields.

The aim of this chapter is to inspire and motivate readers on their journey towards personal growth and self-love. It showcases how these influential figures use positive affirmations and insightful words to overcome challenges, achieve their goals, and maintain a positive outlook on life.

Each affirmation or quote is accompanied by a brief discussion of its meaning and how it can be applied in daily life. This chapter serves as a valuable resource for readers seeking inspiration and guidance in their personal growth journey. It emphasizes the power of words and the impact they can have on our mindset and actions.

Remember, "Words have energy and power with the ability to help, to heal, to hinder, to hurt, to harm, to humiliate, and to humble." (Yehuda Berg) So, let's harness this power for positive change.

COGNITIVE BEHAVIOUR THERAPY (CBT) QUOTES

CBT is based on the principle that thoughts influence feelings, feelings influence behaviours, and behaviours influence our life circumstances. In other words, situations or other people don't make us feel certain ways. It's how we interpret situations or things people say or do that influences how we feel."

CBT has become the evidence-based: treatment of choice for a huge range of problems. It's a practical, problem-solving type of psychological therapy."

CBT helps people understand their problems: and create solutions, by looking at the interaction between their thoughts (cognitions), emotions, behaviours and physiology."

CBT is a form of therapy: that involves examining cognitions or perceptions and how these cognitions relate to patterns of behaviour. CBT is structured, often short-term treatment that is goal-oriented and focused on addressing specific problems or symptoms."

AFFRIMATIONS
QUOTES

- Attitude is a choice. Happiness is a choice. Optimism is a choice. Kindness is a choice. Giving is a choice. Respect is a choice. Whatever choice you make makes you. Choose wisely."
- Don't be pushed around by the fears in your mind. Be led by the dreams in your heart."
- Instead of worrying about what you cannot control, shift your energy to what you can create."
- Be the reason someone smiles. Be the reason someone feels loved and believes in the goodness in people.

THE PATH TO SELF – IMPORVEMENT: NAVIGATING THROUGH AFFIRMATIONS AND CBT

"The journey towards healing is a wonderful, exciting journey towards your own wellbeing. You have finally decided to put yourself first from a holistic perspective, you have decided to take charge of your life. Well done, one of the biggest steps you have already accomplished. Now it is important to implement all these affirmations and mottos into your life and make them part of your daily routine.

The second hardest step would be staying committed, but what is important is that the more you practice, the easier and simpler it will become for you to simply implement them without trying to force or make yourself stay motivated and focused in any way. It is never easy to work on yourself, it is challenging and it can be confronting, but once you start, and stay consistent, as well as give yourself some time to get used to the new change, you will be able to master these affirmations and the mottos, subconsciously.

After using these affirmations and mottos, it is really important to be aware that it is not a quick fix, it will take time. As we know with CBT, it takes time to implement new thoughts and alternate them with the old negative thoughts.

The more you practice, you will have a higher chance to create patterns of new thoughts, emotions, behaviour. It will become part of your subconscious, you won't even know that you're doing it, until in time you become aware of your old patterns not being present anymore in your frontal lobe but in your deep subconscious. You might become aware when your friend tells you.

'Hey, you're not second-guessing yourself anymore, I noticed that for a few days now,' or you might notice yourself when you are in a conversation, you are about to say something (which is

part of the old pattern), before you even say it, your mind will send a signal to your mouth, and you might say,

'Oh, I almost second-guessed myself again, but I stopped just in time.'

This is what CBT is and what affirmations can help you with, both working together, with the help of, using Exposure Therapy, which is just living your life, implementing new thoughts, being able to express them and putting yourself out there, will help you in the long run."

self-improvement is indeed a lifelong journey. It requires dedication, perseverance, and patience. But the rewards are immeasurable. As we grow and evolve, we become better versions of ourselves. We learn new skills, gain new insights, and become more resilient. It's a process that never ends, but it's worth every step.

YOUR PATH, YOUR JOURNEY

A road towards your journey is bumpy and long, at times it might feel cold, and depressive but with ever step that you take, it is the change that you make.

YOUR SELF-
REFLECTION
AWAITS YOU

"Fearing the unknown is understandable, but consider the fear of regret if you don't proceed. Focus instead on what you stand to gain when you do proceed."

TRANSFORMATIONS THROUGH SEASONS

Just as roses go through changes with each season, we too experience changes in our lives. These changes - be it victories, losses, joys, or pains - shape us and help us evolve. They help us shed our fears and insecurities, and usher in new ways of thinking. Keep embracing these changes, for they are the stepping stones to becoming the best version of ourselves.

THE PATHWAY OF
SELF- DISCOVERY

"Don't stand in between your desires and wellbeing. Walk through towards your peace and happiness. You will never know what you might gain until you reach the end. Remember, you are the only one who can stand in between yourself. So, step forward, embrace the journey, and discover the endless possibilities that lie ahead.

THE SOLO AND SHARED JOURNEY: REFLECTION ON SELF- DISCOVERY

Embarking on a journey of self-discovery can sometimes feel like a solitary bus ride on a rainy day. There might be moments of solitude, but remember, it's in these quiet times that we often find our deepest insights. And while the journey can be lonely at times, it's not always so. There are times when we share this journey with loved ones, adding warmth and companionship to our travels. So, whether you're taking the bus alone or with company, embrace the journey. After all, every journey, every reflection, brings us one step closer to discovering ourselves." ◇ ◇

YOUR JOURNEY TOWARDS SELF-DISCOVERY AND IMPROVEMENT

From understanding what makes you happy to defining your own success, these questions will provoke thought and inspire personal growth. This book is not just about finding answers, but also about asking the right questions. Start your journey today and discover the unique individual you are meant to be.

"The book is about holistic mottos and affirmations for life. That's why I have decided, obviously, to include holistic questions. These questions will help you in your self-discovery journey but also in general. Ask yourself, reflect, and implement. You're also able to share these with your loved ones, and all of you can get together, have a discussion, and share each other's perceptions. Learn from each other, not just from life."

- Who am I at my core?
- What are my strengths?
- What are my weaknesses and how can I improve on them?
- What are my goals in life?
- What are the things that make me happy?
- What are the things that I would like to change about my life?
- What are the most important relationships in my life and why?

- What does success mean to me?
- What are the lessons I've learned in my life?
- How can I make a positive impact on the world?
- How do I define my self-worth?
- What are the things that make me feel valuable?
- Do I often compare myself to others? How does that affect my self-worth?
- What are the accomplishments that make me proud and contribute to my self-worth?
- How do I handle criticism and how does it affect my self-worth?
- Do I feel worthy of love and respect?
- What are the qualities I possess that I feel are worthy of admiration?
- How does my self-worth affect my relationships with others?
- What steps can I take to improve my self-worth?
- What does self-care mean to me?
- What are my current self-care practices?
- What activities help me recharge and feel at peace?
- How often do I take time for these self-care activities?
- What barriers prevent me from practicing self-care regularly?
- How does my physical health impact my mental and emotional well-being?
- What steps can I take to improve my physical health?
- How do I handle stress and what coping mechanisms can I improve on?
- What positive affirmations can I use to boost my self-esteem?
- How can I better balance my personal and professional life?
- What does resilience mean to me?
- Can I recall a time when I demonstrated resilience? What was the situation and how did I handle it?
- What strategies do I use to cope with stress and adversity?

- How do I recover from setbacks or disappointments?
- What are the resources (people, activities, inner strengths) that help me bounce back from difficulties?
- How can I improve my capacity to handle life's challenges?
- What role does a positive mindset play in my resilience?
- How does my resilience affect my overall well-being?
- What steps can I take to build my resilience?
- How does my resilience influence my goals and aspirations?
- What are my short-term and long-term goals?
- Why are these goals important to me?
- What steps do I need to take to achieve these goals?
- What resources or skills do I need to acquire to reach my goals?
- How do I plan to overcome potential obstacles on my path to achieving my goals?
- How will I measure my progress towards my goals?
- Who can support me in achieving my goals?
- How do my goals align with my values and passions?
- What will success look like when I achieve my goals?
- How will achieving my goals impact my life and the lives of others?
- What does inner peace mean to me?
- What activities or practices help me feel peaceful and calm?
- How do I handle stress and maintain my inner peace?
- What are the things that disrupt my inner peace and how can I manage them?
- How does my inner peace affect my relationships with others?
- What role does self-care play in maintaining my inner peace?
- How can I cultivate a more peaceful mindset?
- What are the barriers to my inner peace and how can I overcome them?
- How does my inner peace influence my overall well-being and

happiness?

- What steps can I take to enhance my inner peace?
- What does self-love mean to me?
- How do I practice self-love in my daily life?
- What are the things I love about myself?
- How does my self-love affect my relationships with others?
- What are the barriers to my self-love and how can I overcome them?
- How does self-love contribute to my overall well-being and happiness?
- What steps can I take to enhance my self-love?
- How does my self-love influence my goals and aspirations?
- What role does self-care play in cultivating self-love?
- How can I be more compassionate and kinder to myself?
- What does self-respect mean to me and how do I practice it?
- How do I show respect towards others in my daily interactions?
- What are the ways in which I demonstrate respect in my relationships?
- How does my level of self-respect influence my relationships with others?
- What are the barriers to showing respect and how can I overcome them?
- How does respect contribute to my overall well-being and happiness?
- What steps can I take to enhance my respect towards myself and others?
- How does my respect towards others influence my goals and aspirations?
- What role does empathy play in cultivating respect?
- How can I be more understanding and respectful of others' perspectives and experiences?

- What does inner strength mean to me?
- Can I recall a time when I demonstrated inner strength and bravery? What was the situation and how did I handle it?
- What are the sources of my inner strength?
- How do I recognize and acknowledge my bravery in challenging situations?
- How does my inner strength help me overcome obstacles and adversities?
- What role does self-confidence play in my inner strength and bravery?
- How can I cultivate more inner strength and bravery?
- How does my inner strength and bravery influence my goals and aspirations?
- What steps can I take to enhance my recognition of my own bravery?
- How does my inner strength and bravery contribute to my self-esteem and self-worth?
- How do I handle failure and what does it teach me about my inner strength?
- What are the personal values that I will never compromise on?
- How do I handle criticism and how does it affect my self-perception?
- What are the personal boundaries that I have set for myself?
- How do I react when my boundaries are crossed?
- What are the self-limiting beliefs that I need to overcome?
- How does my past influence my present and how can I make peace with it?
- What are the things that I need to forgive myself for?
- What are the things that I would like to say to my future self?
- What gives my life meaning and purpose?
- How does my job or career contribute to my sense of purpose?
- What activities or pursuits make me feel most alive and

fulfilled?

- How do my relationships add meaning to my life?
- What impact do I want to have on the world or on the people around me?
- How do my values and beliefs guide me in finding my purpose?
- What are the things I'm most passionate about and how do they add meaning to my life?
- How does personal growth and self-improvement contribute to my life's meaning?
- What legacy do I want to leave behind?
- How can I align my daily actions and decisions with my larger purpose?
- How do I balance my personal and professional life?
- What are the things that I am willing to sacrifice for my dreams?
- How do I handle rejection and failure?
- What are the things that motivate me to get out of bed every morning?
- How do I handle the uncertainties and unpredictability of life?
- What are the things that I need to let go of to move forward in life?
- How do I define success and how does it align with my life's purpose?
- What are the things that I am grateful for and how do they add meaning to my life?

Now when we have finished the questions, I want you to reflect on these questions, even before you start asking yourself. It is important to understand the meaning behind these questions, when you understand the meaning and what the questions represent, you will be able to easily answer them. Self- reflection is important so is self-awareness, pay attention to yourself, your mind, body, heart, how does it react when you read them? how does it all react after you answer them?

Understanding the Questions: Each question is designed to tap into a different aspect of your self-understanding. For instance, questions about your strengths and weaknesses are about self-evaluation, while questions about your goals and aspirations are about self-projection into the future. Understanding the intent behind each question can help you answer them more thoughtfully and honestly.

Self-Awareness: This involves being aware of your thoughts, emotions, and behaviours. When you read these questions, observe your immediate thoughts and feelings. Do they make you uncomfortable? Excited? Nervous? These reactions can tell you a lot about where you are in your journey of self-discovery.

Self-Reflection: This is the process of questioning, analysing, and understanding your own thoughts, emotions, and behaviours. After answering these questions, reflect on your answers. What do they tell you about your values, desires, fears, and insecurities?

Mind, Body, Heart Connection: Pay attention to how your body reacts when you engage with these questions. Do you feel tension, relaxation, or perhaps a rush of energy? Our bodies often hold wisdom about our emotional states that our minds can overlook.

Sharing and Learning: Discussing these questions with loved ones can be a powerful exercise. It allows you to gain different perspectives and learn from others' experiences and insights. It can also deepen your relationships through shared vulnerability and understanding.

'I AM ENOUGH': A RARE REMINDER FROM SELENA GOMES 'I AM ENOUGH

Selena Gomez, a renowned artist and actress, has been open about her journey towards self-confidence and the role of positive affirmations in her life. In an interview with News24 compiled by Bonolo Sekudu, she shared some insights that can inspire us all.

Selena is a big advocate for therapy and positive self-talk. She has a unique practice of keeping sticky notes around her house with positive affirmations written on them. Among these affirmations, one stands out as her Favorite: "**I am enough**". She refers to these affirmations as "rare reminders", a testament to their precious value in her life.

In addition to using affirmations, Selena also emphasizes the importance of taking breaks from social media. This practice helps her maintain a healthy mindset and focus on her personal growth.

Selena's story is a powerful reminder of the impact affirmations can have on our lives. Her Favorite affirmation, "I am enough", resonates with the core belief that we are all inherently worthy. As you read through this book and explore the affirmations within, remember **Selena's "rare reminder". You, too, are enough.**

I AM: A JOURNEY OF SELF – AFFRIMATIONS

"**I** am **Kristina** and this is my journey of self-affirmation. I believe in the power of positive self-talk and affirmations to shape our thoughts, actions, and ultimately, our lives."

"**I am resilient.**" Life has thrown many challenges my way, but each one has only made me stronger. This affirmation reminds me of my ability to bounce back from adversity.

"**I am creative.**" As a writer, creativity is at the heart of what I do. This affirmation fuels my imagination and inspires me to think outside the box.

"**I am deeply grateful** for my innate ability to shape the life I desire. Despite the obstacles that stand in my path, I manifest my dreams with unwavering determination, steadfast commitment, diligent work, and fiery passion. I yearn for this life, not merely as a distant dream, but as a reality within my grasp. I hold an unshakeable belief in my potential to achieve it.

Despite the numerous health and life obstacles I've faced, I've held onto my belief in my ability to create the life I desire. If I can do it, I firmly believe that you can too. Remember, it's important not to be too hard on yourself. Life is a journey with ups and downs, and it's okay to take it one step at a time. Always prioritize self-care and remember, you are capable, you are resilient, and you are enough." Keep this affirmation close to your heart and repeat it as often as you need"

UNPACKING THE
POWER OF
AFFRIMATIONS

I am resilient: Like everyone else, I have experienced numerous hardships in my life. These painful moments have shaped me, but they have not defined me. Instead, they have forged within me a resilience that is as unyielding as it is empowering.

I am a reflective individual, often finding myself in deep thought, feeling beyond the immediate pain and frustration. I reflect on my experiences, learning from each one, growing with each one.

In many ways, I have always been a teacher, a leader, a seeker of life's philosophies. I don't merely exist; I strive to learn from life, to extract wisdom from experiences for my own benefit. This introspective journey has led me to realize profound truths about myself.

I am resilient. I am determined. I am passionate. I am committed.

These are not just words; they are the essence of who I am. They are the pillars upon which I build my life, the principles that guide my journey. And in this journey, I am not alone. I believe that if I can navigate through life's obstacles and manifest my dreams, so can you.

I am creative: From my early teens, I've been captivated by the power of words. I remember penning essays about the philosophy of life, delving into profound analyses that stirred my soul. I would eagerly share my writings with my mother, cherishing her feedback.

As a non-fiction writer specializing in self-help, I've found a unique joy in exploring the philosophy of life from my perspective. It's an experience that's hard to put into words. When I start analysing life and enter my creative mode, I find myself in a state of flow. Days and nights blend together as I write, so engrossed in my work that I often forget to eat or drink. When I finally rise from my chair, I can barely stand, such is the intensity of my immersion.

This is a feeling unlike any other, a moment I wish could last forever. If my body permitted, I would write for weeks, months, even years on end. But I am only human, and I must respect my limits.

Yet, these are the moments I cherish, the moments I wish to freeze in time. They remind me of why I write: not just to express myself, but to lose myself in the realm of words."

Writing is more than just a hobby or a profession for me; it's a passion that burns brightly within my soul. I plan to write for as long as my mind continues to weave words, my heart pulses with passion, and my body allows me to translate my thoughts into text. This is not just a commitment, but a pledge to my own self, to continue doing what I love most. So, here's to a future filled with words, wisdom, and endless possibilities."

I am deeply grateful: I am deeply grateful for the journey that has led me to this moment. I firmly believe that we all possess unique talents and the potential to achieve our dreams. Manifesting these dreams requires not just positive affirmations and attitudes, but also hard work, dedication, determination, passion, and access to resources.

Life is not always easy. At times, it can be harder for some than for others. But we are all human beings, and if something causes you pain, that's what matters. Never feel guilty or belittle your feelings just because someone else might have it worse. You are allowed to feel what you feel.

We all face obstacles in life, whether they be financial, psychological, medical, or stemming from unhealthy relationships or lack of support. Despite these challenges, remember this: You are resilient, even if you don't realize it yet. You are smart and capable.

Like many, I've had my share of personal issues. But I was able to use life experiences, learned lessons, affirmations, and cognitive behaviour therapy, coupled with a strong will, to improve, to feel better, and to strive for the life I've always dreamed of. This journey has led me to where I am today.

With pride, I can say that I am a Family and Relationship Therapist specializing in Trauma and Addiction. I am a Holistic Life Purpose Coach and the founder of my digital business, 'Kristina's Holistic Approach for Your Wellbeing.' And now, I am embarking on a new journey as a first-time author with this book.

Reflecting back, it wasn't easy. But I learned not to give up. I learned to take a break when things got hard, and I wasn't feeling motivated or creative. I learned to listen to my mind and body, to slow down, and not to push myself too hard. Sometimes, what you want to achieve doesn't always come when you want it. Sometimes, it comes when you least expect it.

I believe that a strong desire for the life you want is the biggest driving force in your achievements. It's important to have a vision and not lose sight of it. That vision is your map. Remember, your vision can change over time. The more you experience and try out new things, the more you will learn about yourself, and your vision will evolve.

I believe that you can achieve everything you want. Believe in yourself, take time when needed, hold onto your vision, and don't let life or others sway you from your chosen path. Remember, it's all part of experiencing and finding out about yourself through life's experiences, trials, and errors."

Remember, your journey is unique to you. Embrace it, learn from it, and most importantly, believe in yourself.

EMPOWERING WORDS: MY JOURNEY AS AN AUTHOR

Every author has a unique story to tell, not just through their books, but also through their personal journey in the world of writing. I am no exception. In this chapter, I want to share a bit about my work, the type of author I am, and why it's so important to me.

I see myself as more than just an author. I am a motivator, an inspirer, an empowered. Through my words, I strive to uplift, to encourage, and to ignite a spark within my readers. I believe in the power of words to transform lives, and I consider it a privilege to be able to contribute to that transformation.

My work is a reflection of my passion for helping others. Whether it's through my role as a Family and Relationship Therapist, a Holistic Life Purpose Coach, or as the founder of 'Kristina's Holistic Approach For Your Wellbeing', my goal is always to inspire and empower.

As an author, I bring this same passion to my writing. I pour my heart and soul into every word, every sentence, every page. My hope is that my readers can feel this passion and be inspired by it.

But it's not just about inspiring others. It's also about inspiring myself. Writing is a journey of self-discovery, of personal growth. It's a way for me to explore my thoughts, my feelings, my experiences. It's a way for me to express who I am and who I aspire to be.

So, as you read this book, know that it's more than just a collection of words on a page. It's a piece of my heart, a glimpse into my soul. It's a testament to my belief in the power of positive affirmations, and my hope that they can make a difference in your life, just as they have in mine.

In my work I've had the privilege of witnessing firsthand the transformative power of positive affirmations and a resilient mindset. I've seen how they can help individuals overcome challenges, achieve their goals, and lead more fulfilling lives.

Whether it's helping someone navigate through a difficult period in their life, or guiding them towards realizing their full potential, my work has shown me the incredible strength and resilience that lies within each of us.

This book is a culmination of those experiences. It's a testament to the power of positive thinking, and a guide to help you harness that power for yourself."

As I continue on my journey as an author, I am excited about the projects that lie ahead. I am currently working on several new books, each with its own unique message and purpose. These books will delve deeper into the themes of self-discovery, resilience, and empowerment, offering new insights and perspectives. Each of these books is a Labor of love, a testament to my commitment to inspiring and empowering my readers. As with all my work, I am pouring my heart and soul into these projects, striving to create content that resonates, inspires, and makes a difference.

So, as you turn the last page of this book, know that this is not the end, but merely the beginning. There are many more empowering words to come, many more stories to tell. I invite you to join me on this journey, to grow with me, to be inspired, and to discover the power within you.

Keep an eye out for my future books, and together, let's continue this journey of empowerment and transformation."

A NOTE OF THANKS AND ENCOURAGEMENT

"If you've chosen to read this book, I want to take a moment to say thank you. Your decision to pick up this book signifies your interest in personal growth and development. It shows that you are invested in healing yourself, that you love and value yourself enough to take this step. Remember, you are worth it. You deserve the best. This journey you're embarking on is a testament to your strength and resilience. It's a testament to your willingness to embrace change, to strive for better, to never stop growing. So, as you delve into the pages of this book, know that each word is written with you in mind. Each chapter is a stepping stone on your path to empowerment. And remember, this is not just a book, it's a journey.

A journey that you are about to embark on, filled with self-discovery and personal growth. As you turn each page, may you find the courage to face your fears, the strength to overcome your challenges, and the wisdom to understand your worth.

Remember, this journey is not a race, but a process. It's okay to take your time, to pause and reflect, to absorb and understand. This book is a tool, a guide, but the real change comes from within you.

So, thank you for taking this step, for choosing to invest in yourself. You are brave, you are strong, and you are capable. As you embark on this journey, remember to be kind to yourself, to be patient with your progress, and to celebrate every small victory.

Here's to your journey of self-discovery and personal growth. May it be enlightening, enriching, and empowering. Good luck!"

NOTE FOR MY
LOVELY READERS

As a first-time author, I've always known the type of writer I wanted to be - one who uses her words to heal, empower, and make a difference in your life. I sincerely hope that I was able to achieve this with this book.

Remember, you matter. You have only one life, so work hard to improve yourself and do your best to enjoy life. Focus on the good things, the things you can control, and the things that make you happy. When you find yourself worrying or stressing, remember that your health matters. Make priorities and ask yourself, "Is this worry worth it? Is this stress worth it?" Focus on what matters and what you can control.

As a therapist and a holistic purpose coach, I have personally used Cognitive Behavioural Therapy (CBT) with my clients and on myself. Believe me when I tell you this, CBT and affirmations are effective in due time and supported with evidence, but you also have to give your best. Change is a process, and it's okay to take it one step at a time.

I have seen and experienced change not just in myself but in my wonderful, inspirational, and brave clients. Their journeys have been a testament to the power of self-discovery and personal growth.

The Power of Affirmations

Affirmations are more than just positive statements. They are powerful tools that can help you challenge and overcome self-sabotaging and negative thoughts. When you repeat them often and believe in them, you can start to make positive changes in your life.

In this book, we've explored various affirmations that can help you navigate your thoughts and emotions. These affirmations are not just words on a page, but practical strategies that you can incorporate into your daily life. They can help you create a positive mindset, boost your self-esteem, and cultivate a sense of self-love.

The Role of Cognitive Behavioural Therapy

Cognitive Behavioural Therapy (CBT) is more than just a type of psychotherapy. It's a tool that can help you understand and change thought patterns that lead to harmful actions or distressing feelings. It can be a very helpful tool in treating mental health disorders, such as depression, post-traumatic stress disorder (PTSD), and eating disorders.

As a therapist, I have seen the transformative power of CBT firsthand. It's not just a theoretical concept, but a practical tool that can bring about significant change in one's life. By understanding the impact of our thoughts on our feelings and behaviours, we can learn to challenge negative thought patterns and replace them with healthier, more positive ones.

Embracing the Journey

Here's wishing you a successful journey of self-discovery and personal growth. Remember, you are capable of more than you know. As you turn the last page of this book, know that your journey doesn't end here. In fact, it's just beginning. The road to self-discovery is a lifelong journey, and I'm honoured to have been a part of yours.

As we conclude this book, I want to remind you that the journey of self-discovery is not always easy. There will be challenges and obstacles along the way. But remember, every challenge is an opportunity for growth. Every obstacle is a stepping stone to becoming a better version of yourself.

So, as you close this book and continue on your journey, remember to be patient with yourself. Change takes time. But with persistence and determination, you can overcome any challenge that comes your way.